The
PEACE
BELL

by Margi Preus

illustrated by Hideko Takahashi

Henry Holt and Company
New York

The author would like to thank Shoji Wakako and
the Shoji family in Japan, the Duluth Sister Cities Program,
and the many people who contributed information for this story.

The illustrator would like to thank Saitou Koji, Sase Miyoko,
and Tsuchiya Yoji of Ohara, Japan, for a tour and information on the
Peace Bell, and to Jim Leuci for information on U.S. Navy uniforms.

Henry Holt and Company, LLC
Publishers since 1866
175 Fifth Avenue
New York, New York 10010
www.HenryHoltKids.com

Library of Congress Cataloging-in-Publication Data
Preus, Margi.
The Peace Bell / Margi Preus ; illustrated by Hideko Takahashi.—1st ed.
p.   cm.
Summary: Yuko's grandmother tells about how the bell in their town
that would ring on New Year's Eve is given up during the war for scrap metal,
finds its way back to their village and becomes known as the Peace Bell.
ISBN-13: 978-0-8050-7800-8
ISBN-10: 0-8050-7800-2
[1. Bells—Fiction. 2. Grandmothers—Fiction. 3. New Year—Fiction. 4. Friendship—Fiction.
5. Japan—History—20th century—Fiction.] I. Takahashi, Hideko, ill. II. Title.
PZ7.P92434Pe 2008   [E]—dc22   2007040897

First Edition—2008
Book design by Laurent Linn
The artist used Japanese acrylic paints on illustration board
to create the illustrations for this book.
Printed in the United States of America on acid-free paper. ∞

1 3 5 7 9 10 8 6 4 2

To the people of Ohara
and to peacemakers everywhere
—M. P.

To Aunt Takahashi Suzuko, Uncle Takahashi Yuji,
and my parents, Takahashi Yozo and Yoshie,
with thanks for sharing memories for this book
—H. T.

Yuko and I run along ahead of her grandmother
on the lane that leads through the bright green rice.
     We are going to see something special. It's special
for Yuko because she lives here in Japan, and for me,
Katie-chan, because I am visiting from America.
Yuko's grandmother says it's important to her, too.
As we climb the hill into the cool shade of the tall
trees, she tells us this story.

Long ago, when I was your age, I loved the pale, gentle beauty of the cherry blossoms.

I loved the big, deep *BOOM* of the Bon Odori drum.

I loved the moon rising round and full over the ocean. Even though it was so far away, it seemed close enough to touch.

But most of all I loved the deep *KA-DOON* of an ancient temple bell. Its song was as gentle as cherry blossoms, as deep as the Bon Odori drum, and as round and full as the moon.

New Year's Eve was my favorite day of the year. On that evening our family slurped up bowls of *toshi-koshi soba*—long-life noodles—and went to the temple. The grounds swirled with women in colorful new kimonos and men sipping cups of hot sake. But everyone was quiet, waiting for the ringing of the temple bell.

At the stroke of midnight, the bell began to sing.
KA-DOON, it sang, again and again—
Twelve for the twelve months,
Twenty-four for the twenty-four atmospheres,
Seventy-two for the seventy-two climates of the earth.
    One hundred and eight times in all, each toll chasing away one of the one hundred and eight worries of the world. And when it ended, the song of the bell kept ringing inside me.

The war soon followed and there weren't any
more joyous New Year celebrations. There were
no new kimonos because of shortages. Sometimes
there weren't any noodles for the soup!

Even the bell was gone.

"Gone to Tokyo or Yokosuka," the women in the fish market said. "Donated to the war effort." Every town was expected to donate metal for the war.

"Will it come back when the war is over?" I asked.

"Oh, no," said the woman selling eels. "The bell won't ever come back. It will be melted down and made into gun barrels or shell casings."

I frowned. I knew it was important to support the war, but it seemed wrong to make a peaceful bell into weapons. "The war will end, the soldiers will come home, and the bell will come back, too," I said.

I tried to sing a cheerful song, but it stuck in my throat.

As the war went on, nobody sang anymore.

The rain hissed, *shito shito*.

The distant thunder grumbled, *goro goro*.

The train leaving the station sighed, *sayonara*—
good-bye.

And though I tried to hold the song of the bell
close to me, it was so far away that not even an
echo remained.

The war finally ended, but people weren't any happier.

Once a truck full of American soldiers rumbled through town. Everyone ran into their houses to hide, except my friends and I who were caught outside. We held our breath and tried to look invisible.

The soldiers waved and threw candy, but we were too afraid to pick it up. When they were gone, there was just the sound of cicadas screeching in the summer heat.

Then, little by little and yet somehow suddenly,
our town sprang to life. Trucks trundled by carrying
lumber. New roads were built, and shops and homes
sprouted up alongside them.

My ears filled up with giggling and chattering,
and my nose with the delicious lunchtime smells
of fish cakes and pickled plums.

Years passed and my heart began to fill up, too.
Soon my mother was clucking and cooing over me
as she tucked me into the kimono I would wear
for my wedding.

Later I clucked and cooed over my own baby daughter. But there was still an empty spot in my heart where the bell's song used to live.

Then one day in the fish market, I heard the
women say, "The bell is coming back! That old
temple bell—the Americans are sending it back!"

"How do the Americans have our bell?" I asked.

"Some American sailors found it in a Yokosuka
shipyard and took it all the way to Minn-ee-so-ta."

"But why are they sending it back?"

"To be friendly, I think."

All day long my bicycle tires hummed,
and so did I.

What a celebration there was when the bell came home! A parade wove through town, with drums and flutes playing, children in bright kimonos waving flags, and the bell riding in a cart like an emperor. There were songs and dances and many long speeches.

The bell was named the Peace Bell and placed in a
brand-new *shoro,* or bell tower, in a special hilltop park.

After many long years of silence, the bell was allowed to have its say. *KA-DOON* it sang, in a voice as gentle as cherry blossoms, as deep as the Bon Odori drum, and as round and full as the moon.

It sang away all the years of sorrow.

It sang of new friendships to come.

And it sang of the hope for peace in the hearts of people all over the world.

"Obah-chan," Yuko whispers to her grandmother, "could a bell really tell you all that?"

"Everything has something to say," Yuko's grandmother says, "if you know how to listen."

Just then, we step out of the trees into a small clearing where a big bell hangs in a red tower.

"Here is the very bell, the bell that lived in Katie-chan's town in Minnesota for some years. Go ahead, ring it!"

I take the rope in my hands, but even before I hear
the first KA-DOON, I know the song. Or at least I feel
it, gentle and deep and round and full.

I feel it in my heart.

A NOTE ABOUT THE STORY

Thousands of Japanese temple bells were donated to the war effort during World War II. These bells were treated as scrap metal and were melted down and remade into materials needed for the war. Some of the donated bells survived; a few were returned to their original cities. Although the story told here is fictional, it is inspired by the true story of two towns, one in Japan and one in America.

Sometime during the war, the town of Ohara in Japan donated a bell from an abandoned temple. Until 1946, the bell sat untouched in a Yokosuka shipyard. No one knows why the bell escaped unscathed, but it was discovered intact by navy crew members from the U.S.S. *Duluth,* when they were stationed in Japan after the war.

The crew presented the bell as a gift to the ship's namesake, Duluth, a small city on the shores of Lake Superior, in Minnesota. For eight years it sat in dignified silence in Duluth's City Hall, with no way of being sounded. Then a visiting Japanese professor heard of the bell and began an investigation of its origins. It was discovered that the bell had been crafted by a famous artisan in the year 1686. By examining the names of prominent citizens engraved on the bell, it was also determined that it had originated from the town known then as Ohara, Chiba Prefecture.

As a gesture of goodwill, Duluth returned the bell to Ohara in early May 1954. Amid much fanfare, the bell was renamed the American-Japanese Friendship Peace Bell and was placed on the summit of a hill that during the war had served as both bomb shelter and lookout. A sister-city relationship began between the two cities in 1989, and in 1991 Ohara presented Duluth with a replica of the bell, which now hangs in a specially crafted *shoro* in a beautiful hilltop park.

Although Yuko's grandmother is a fictional character, her spirit is alive in the people of Ohara (now called Isumi City), who welcome visitors from Duluth every year. A warm relationship continues between the two cities.